LETTERING

Beginners Guide to Lettering and Calligraphy for DIY, Crafts, and Art

Sandra Williams

Sandra Williams

Disclaimer Notice:

Please note the information contained within this document is for educational and entertainment purposes only. Every attempt has been made to provide accurate, up to date and reliable complete information. No warranties of any kind are expressed or implied. Readers acknowledge that the author is not engaging in the rendering of legal, financial, medical or professional advice.

By reading this document, the reader agrees that under no circumstances are we responsible for any losses, direct or indirect, which are incurred as a result of the use of information contained within this document, including, but not limited to, — errors, omissions, or inaccuracies.

Table of Contents

Introduction

I want to thank you and congratulate you for purchasing the book, "Lettering: Beginners Guide to Lettering and Calligraphy for DIY, Crafts, and Art".

This book contains proven steps and strategies on how to become a successful calligrapher, even though you are just new to calligraphy. It shows you all the methods that you need to employ to begin to create some calligraphic masterpieces that you can share with friends or use for special occasions.

Researches reveal that the art of calligraphy started almost 5000 years ago. Today, even with the emergence of computers and other technologies that could replace calligraphy or the art of writing beautifully, it still thrives. By the looks of it, calligraphy is here to stay even if more people find typing a lot easier than writing. Why? It is simply because a thing of beauty is meant to last forever. Indeed, calligraphy is a beautiful thing. It's a way of expressing yourself and showing that you want to present something with great care.

In this book, you will learn about the history of calligraphy, discover the secrets to becoming a successful calligrapher, know the latest trends, find out how you can earn profits and start a career with this art plus so much more. Prepare yourself to enjoy a new pastime because once you get that quill in your hand, you won't want to put it down. In fact, you will spend your time deciding on new and exciting ways in which you can use your newly acquired skill.

Thanks again for purchasing this book, and it is hoped that the information you glean from it will help you to use your creative style in producing masterpieces of your own. Calligraphy is such a wonderful craft and there are so many applications that you can use it for, as you will see in the pages of the chapters that lie ahead.

Section 1

Introduction to Calligraphy and Font Styles

Sandra Williams

Chapter 1

Calligraphy at a Glance

The word calligraphy came from the Ancient Greek words "kallos" meaning beautiful and "graphe" meaning writing. Calligraphy is, therefore, more than just ordinary lettering or handwriting. It is an art that gives form to letters and signs in an expressive, skillful and well balanced manner. The visual art has confident strokes and proportion that the only way to describe it is "strikingly beautiful".

Thousands of years ago, calligraphy was used for monuments through cutting letters in stones. This was a very slow and difficult process. Books such as the Bible, Chaucer's Canterbury Tales, other Greek and Latin texts and love declarations between King Arthur and Queen Guinevere were produced the same way. Imagine the length of time it took for a single book to be completed. Today, there are millions of books being published in a year. Various fonts and styles are utilized. With the technology of today, one can have a book in a matter of hours or days.

A Short History on Calligraphy

When and how did calligraphy start? Nobody can really tell. It was estimated to have come more than 4000 years ago, after the invention of language in China. Archaeological discoveries include a jar with a painting of a sunrise believed to be created by the primitive Chinese around 4000-2000 BC.

Western calligraphy, on the other hand, is believed to have started during the Roman times. This is where calligraphy is said to have reached its height of beauty. Aside from cutting letters in stones, the Romans used to write simple messages using a metal stylus and wax tablets or a feather or pen with ink on a tree bark. It was very difficult to decipher the letters written on barks though, as the letters were not well formed and they seemed to overlap with one another. Hence, a writing style, known as Uncial, was developed. From there, other writing styles emerged.

Uncial script 1407

Different Writing Styles

Uncial. The early English adapted this type of lettering style. This type used capital letters only. Uncial was very common during the 4th to 8th centuries AD. The Latin and Greek scribes mostly used Uncial for religious writings. The main problem with this style was that it took a great deal of space since the letters were round and wide. However, since this style was utilized mostly for religious purposes, the people did not mind that problem.

The Romans borrowed this style and named it uncial, which meant an inch. Although the height of the letters was far from being an inch each, still the name prevailed.

Half-uncials. This style of writing was easier to use compared to uncial. It became popular around the 6th century, especially among the Christian churches. For ceremonies or events of a religious nature, the half-uncial style was utilized. This type used lower case, unlike the uncials, which were all in upper case.

Insular Minuscule. This style was developed around the 7th century, closely related to both the uncials and half-uncial writings. With this style, the first letter of the word was very big and the succeeding letters decreased in size until the normal size of the letter was reached. Another special feature is that letters with ascenders (examples are letters b, d, and h) were written with triangular tops or sometimes, wedge-shaped tops. On the other hand, letters with descenders, such as g, p, and q, had elaborate and long tails.

Caroline Minuscule. This style of writing shortened the ascenders and descenders and lessened the slant of the letters. Hence, it was easier to read and the letters looked grander. It was developed during the reign of Emperor Charlemagne. Its outstanding feature was its legibility. Afterwards, the English Caroline Minuscule Compressed style was developed. This allowed more letters to be written per line. However, some complained that the words became more difficult to decipher.

Gothic Black Letter. This style is known for its thin and thick strokes. This was best used for titles, headings or logos. This type was very difficult to read when used for the body of the book.

Italics. This style is very popular even today. It slants slightly to the right. This is used to give emphasis to certain words or when stating a quotation or quoting the words of a speaker. Its name was given to honor Italy, where beautiful and artistic typesetters were first designed.

Today, there are hundreds of writing styles that one can choose from. Not only that, you can easily learn the art of calligraphy whether your handwriting is good or not. Plus, you will discover that calligraphy can be more than just a hobby. It is a potential income-generating art. Find out more about calligraphy as you read on. In no time at all, you will be producing your own scrolls, artwork and signs and will be able to share these with friends.

The old fashioned idea of producing lettering by the use of calligraphy may have been the only way to produce the written word when it was invented. However, modern technology has many opportunities to offer you with alphabets coming in printable sheets, that you can use to style the work that you do. The monks of old did not have all the benefits that we do now. The colors of inks are diverse, the materials available are diverse and at least we have decent light in which to work when preparing out calligraphic masterpieces.

Read on to find out how you can help to be part of this history by keeping the traditional alive.

Quidã eius libros nõ ipſius eſſe ſed Dionyſii &Zophiri co
lophoniorũ tradunt:qui iocãdi cauſa cõſcribentes ei ut diſ
ponere idoneo dederunt.Fuerunt autẽ Menippi ſex. Prius
qui de lydis ſcripſit:Xanthũq; breuiauit.Secũdus hic ipſe.
Tertius ſtratonicus ſophiſta.Quartus ſculptor. Quintus
& ſextus pictores:utroſq; memorat apollodorus.Cynici au
tem uolumina tredecĩ ſunt.Neniæ:teſtamenta:epiſtolæ cõ
poſitæ ex deorum pſona ad phyſicos & mathematicos grã⁄
maticoſq;:& epicuri fœtus:& eas quæ ab ipſis religioſe co⁄
luntur imagines:& alia.

Calligraphy from 1470

Chapter 2

The Secrets to Becoming a Success in Calligraphy

There are schools that offer calligraphy short courses or even degree programs. Some professional organizations also hold seminars on calligraphy. Sometimes, these seminars are even free. Watch out for such offers. These are great opportunities to learn tactics and a variety of techniques to become a good calligrapher. However, how about those who were not given the opportunities to have an education or attend seminars? Could they still become good calligraphers?

The good news is that those who did not have the luxury of education could still be successful in this career. Here are some keys on becoming a successful calligrapher.

1. Love for the art. Calligraphy is more of a thing of the heart than the hand. Yes, it is undeniable that one could become

successful when one is skilled in writing. However, practice, dedication, commitment, willingness to learn, among other things, would require one's heart to fulfill the requirements of becoming a good, and especially, a great calligrapher. It would also be the love or passion for this art that would push you to continue when you are on the verge of giving up.

2. Patience. Calligraphy can be frustrating. Just like other forms of art, one would need so much time and effort to perfect the art. One letter could mean a hundred strokes before you could perfect it. Take note however that even when you have perfected it, you could still commit errors. A word is made up of several letters and just one wrong letter could ruin the whole work. Hence, you must have the virtue of patience. Becoming a great calligrapher can take years. Do you have the patience for that?

3. Eye for details. The letters may have similarities but each one is unique. The calligrapher must have keen eyes to notice the difference. How thin or thick each letter is also important. Every small line or curve is significant. The height of each letter matters, too. These may seem like small things for other people but one who has plans on

making a career out of calligraphy should possess this quality.

4. Excellence. Writing is not the same as writing beautifully. Calligraphy is an art that requires excellence. The main goal is mastery of the art and not just knowledge on how to do calligraphy. Be creative, too. Open your mind and eyes to numerous possibilities.

5. Practice. This will separate the good from the best. How many hours and efforts you give to this art will determine how well you become. There is no short cut to this.

6. More practice. One cannot overemphasize the importance of this key in becoming a good calligrapher. Spend every free time trying to perfect the art. It must become a part of your daily routine. You must give time to it. You have to provide a schedule to it. You do not do it when you have extra time to spare. It is the other way around. If this is important to you, you must prioritize it over other things.

7. Materials. The tools and supplies for calligraphy are important factors in the acquisition of this skill. However, one can become a good calligrapher whether one's material is complete or not. Materials could make practice easier but it is not really mandatory. If you have the means,

then invest in quality materials. If not, a ballpoint or felt-tip pens would do for starters. These would not be able to employ angled lines, however. Here are some of the materials that you need:

a. Pens – flat-balled or round-nibbed pens. You could avail of multi-nibbed pens for more elaborate decorations or designs of fonts. Nib is the part of the dip or the fountain pen that touches the paper. There are many shapes, sizes and types of nibs. You would not need them all. Smaller ones are more frequently used than the bigger ones.

b. Calligraphy markers – these have flat or angled tips. They are used for special calligraphy lettering.

c. Brush – Steel brushes are sometimes used in adding decorative lines to the fonts.

d. Writing ink – preferable is water-based ink as this is less vicious than oil-based inks.

e. High quality paper – popularly used are parchment or vellum. These papers do not need a light box as one can achieve straight lines even without the use of pencil markings. In addition, in the event that an error is committed, one can simply use a knife to erase imperfections with these papers. Ruled paper is used for beginners to serve as a guideline for the height of the letters.

f. Rulers – a light table is better but more expensive in guiding you to have that perfect height and spacing in writing. Another great tool is graph paper to practice. The most practical tool, however, is ruler. Use this to make lettering guidelines. The ruler should be transparent and try to have the different lengths of rulers.

g. Pencil and eraser. Very useful during your practice sessions and while you are just learning the different styles of writing.

h. Develop a portfolio. Try to gather and preserve all your works as this can be used when you are applying for a job or starting your own business n calligraphy.

i. Be a member of a professional organization. Examples are the Society of Scribes and the Society for Calligraphy. If you are a member, you have opportunities to attend workshops and seminars and meet other calligraphers plus you would be updated on the latest trends and news on calligraphy, among other things.

j.   Belief in yourself. Trust that you will become a good calligrapher in time. It may not look like it, you may not feel it but it would happen when you think you can. Have a positive mindset and attitude and you are halfway there.

Anybody could be a successful calligrapher. One is not born as a master calligrapher. One could start from scratch and end up as a great calligrapher, but it will take all of the attributes shown above and the first step of all is practice.

Once you have read the book, get yourself an exercise book and a calligraphy pen because it's time to choose the fonts or texts that you like and learn how to transfer these onto the lines of your exercise book. Think of it as drawing, rather than writing because that's what it's all about.

The biggest secret to becoming a success at calligraphy is to experiment with new lettering all of the time. Take time to try more complex lettering because it's very satisfying and the more complex letters can be used as openings to your text.

It is worthwhile to have some resource books of different styles and the best collection that you can have is made by Dover as these are copyright free lettering that will help you to expand your portfolio of styles and make your work stand out from the crowd.

The book that I use on a regular basis is 100 Calligraphic Alphabets and this is a great text book to have to help you with your calligraphy practice. There are some great fonts shown in this book which are useful and which will help you to increase your possibility of variation while creating individual artworks that use calligraphy as their main feature.

Sandra Williams

Chapter 3
It's all about the Fonts

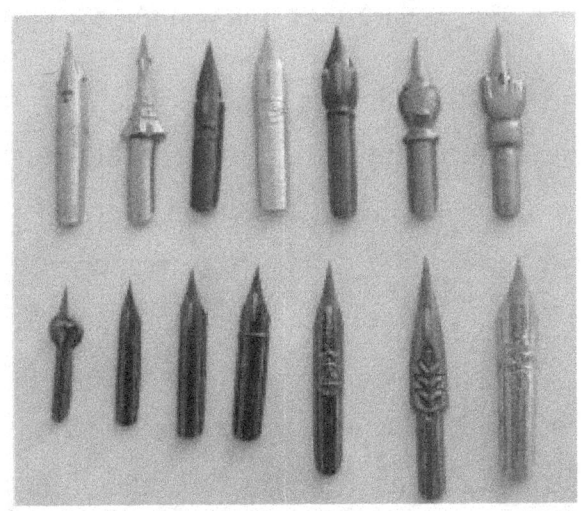

Calligraphy nibs

Calligraphy and fonts are inseparable. What is a font? It is a set of text characters with a specific design or style, size, width, slant, and ornamentation that can be printed or displayed. It includes letters, numbers, punctuation marks and other characters that would make up a typeface.

What is a font? It is everything. It could reveal your personality. It could tell if you're in a happy, sad, serious or playful mood. It is a message on its own. You may try to relay a message saying "I like you" but a dark, thick, ugly, creepy design of a font could change your message in an instant. A font could make or break a message. Hence, selecting the right font is essential. Here are some tips you can follow to have the correct font for your project, business, love letter, or whatever it is you need.

- Make sure that it fits the occasion. Your foremost consideration is the nature of event that you will use the font to. It is similar to choosing a wardrobe. If you were going to a wedding, you would pick something formal, right? You would not wear a pair of jeans, definitely. The same thing goes when choosing fonts. What is the occasion? Is it a formal event or not? If it is formal, then the font should be straight with rounded forms. Script is popular among formal invitations for weddings, diplomas or special occasions. It is like a cursive handwriting with artistic curves and strokes. Nowadays, there are also fonts that can describe exactly how you feel. For instance, you can make your message colorful to emphasize how happy you are currently feeling. Serious fonts are straight, black and simple. There are no special arts or designs to them. You can send a note showing whether you feel hot or cold. The fonts could look either frozen or on fire. Whether you feel angry or not, the recipients would be able to tell. The fonts could do the talking for you.

- Group the fonts accordingly. There would be times that you would need to use different fonts in one message. For instance, a wedding invitation. In the first page, there could be the details of the wedding. Then, in the next page, there is the list of the entourage. Perhaps in the last page, there is the map for the venue or other instructions. If this were the scenario, you would need to know what font to use per page as you cannot use the same font all throughout the invitation. It would simply be inappropriate. The elegance of the invitation would depend on how well you can coordinate the different fonts. Again, similar to choosing your wardrobe, try to stick to the overall theme. You would not pair a formal top with a summer shorts, would you? In the same manner, do not try to mix and match formal and informal fonts in one project. Find the appropriate fonts that go well together. Here is the rule – keep it the same, stick to the theme.

- How to do contrast? If there is really a need to have contrasting fonts in a single page, for example in making a grade school newspaper, the contrast should really be sharp and obvious. Say that the cartoon section and the announcement are placed in one page. The fonts should have a definite contrast that would not leave the readers wondering if the two sections are together or not. Using the appropriate contrast could help shift the mood of the readers accordingly. A good example is Helvetica and Bembo. These two contrasting fonts could be placed in one page and the result would not be awkward.

- How to use that special font? Everybody has his or her own favorite font. If the occasion is not that formal and your favorite font would look awesome on your message, then by all means, use it. However, here is one important tip. Use that special font to the most important part of the letter or invitation. Never use it throughout the entire project. Doing so would remove its being "special".

- Follow your heart. There may be do's and don'ts but the final authority when choosing the font to use is your heart. Listen to your instinct. Do not be afraid to experiment. On top of all these tips, calligraphy should be fun. It is an enjoyable thing to do.

With that, it is time to choose the fonts now. As mentioned, there are literally hundreds of fonts to choose from. When you see the word serif, it refers to the small decorative line of a letter or character of a font. The most common example is the Times Roman font. Sans-serif means the absence of such line with Helvetica as the example.

ABCDEFGHIJKLMN
ÑOPQRTSUVWXYZ
abcdefghijklmnñopqr
stuvwxyzàéî&$
1234567890

Ever wonder which are the top 10 most popular fonts? Here is the list.

- New Baskerville. Named after its designer John Baskerville in 1757, the strength of this font is its legibility, simplicity and beauty. It possesses the appearance of both the classical and modern look.

- Helvetica —Max Miedinger designed this famous font in 1957, with some help from Edouard Hoffmann. It has a compact appearance that has a wide variety of usage.

- Open Sans. They call this font as the new Arial. It is a very versatile font. You can either use it for headlines or for the body of the article. It works well for formal or informal occasions, too.

- Akzidenz Grotesk. Although it was released in 1896, its rise to popularity occurred during the 1950's. Akzidenz Grotesk influenced the creations of the now-popular Helvetica and Univers fonts. This sans-serif font was widely used in publications in Germany decades ago.

- DIN – developed during 1931, this font remains popular today because of its two strong characteristics – simplicity and beauty. It can be used in various projects and articles. It is also widely used online as users find this font gentle to the eyes, with its soft curves and rounded details.

- Franklin Gothic – It projects power, confidence and boldness. These qualities make this font popular for headlines, books and billboards.

- Gotham 2000 – It was named as the most popular font for designers in the last decade. It is a clean and a modern looking sans serif type of font. It was rumored to be Obama's favorite font as this was the font used during his 2008 campaign.

- Gill Shadow – a very legible sans serif, this font is a combined effort of Eric Gills and Stanley Morrison during the late 1920's. The distinguishing characteristics of Gill Shadows are its pronounced contrast in weight plus the distinct character of each font.

- Futura – designed by Paul Renner in 1927, this geometric sans serif font became popular because of its efficiency and forwardness. This is also commonly used in online articles.

- Roboto – a sans serif that looks like a combination of Helvetica and Din. It is great for everyday articles and projects.

As you pursue calligraphy, whether as a hobby or a new source of extra income, learn about the different fonts available. Appreciate each stroke and curve. Have lots of scratch paper with you and do some free handwriting during your free time. Be adventurous and try to experiment scribbling different fonts. Imagine yourself as a calligrapher and try to invent new designs of fonts. Who can tell? Maybe, your design would be included in the next top ten most popular fonts.

It's a good idea also to have an exercise book on the go at all times, so that when you have a moment to practice, you can. Lined paper works the best because you can use the lines as guides. You can also use a pencil and ruler to create the slope that you want to your lettering, so that all of your letters are consistent and fit in with your scheme.

Look at all of the type sets that are used in Word or your Word processing software as there will be a lot there to help you to choose the style you are best suited to.

Section 2

Practical Application Using Calligraphy

In this section you will learn all the different techniques of using calligraphy for your projects. The section deals with how to practice your calligraphy and to use it for small and larger projects.

It takes you through the processes and also gives you a lot of tips that will be useful to you. This section is where you actually get to practice your calligraphy and take it to another level.

Image copyright: Creative commons attribution: WeLoveit.com

Sandra Williams

Chapter 4
Learning to Practice Calligraphy

Before you begin, you need to gather all of your equipment together. There's nothing worse than sitting down to concentrate on calligraphy and finding that you have something missing. For your practice, we will take various alphabets and go through the process of producing the lettering that makes up that alphabet. There are different strokes needed with your wide nib calligraphy pen and you will need parchment, a ruler, a pencil, your calligraphy pen, a print out of the alphabet that you are to use showing all the letters in big and small letters, tracing paper and of course ink. You can use ink of different colors if you wish to although when practicing black is a good color because it shows you clearly what you place onto the paper.

Let's look at the construction of letters because this will help you to hold your pen correctly. Wherever you have a fat line, your nib is flat against the paper and the movement of the pen is straight. Now try and experiment. Put your pen onto the paper and draw a letter M holding your pen very straight while you draw it. There should be no movement of the nib. This discipline is quite hard to come to terms with but once you get it, you will see that the position of the nib is paramount. As you turn a corner on an M, you will note that the downward swoops should use the full nib, whereas the cross section at the top should use the nib sideways and thus produce a thinner line.

Instead of thinking of writing the M in a traditional way, try it this way because you will find it much easier. Create the M in the traditional way and then add the tops and bottom tails so that your M is as shown above. All of this is good practice. If you want to make letters much bigger, you can simply trace the letters in pencil and then fill them in with pen. Let's take a look at a whole alphabet and you should practice the capitals up to an upper line and keeping all of your smaller letters within the lower line. The best letters to practice your curves are letter such as:

U

See how the line narrows at the bottom. Hold your nib in your hand and start to draw the U from the top left hand side using the broad of the nib. As you reach the curve, keep the broad of the nib straight and the line becomes narrow. Then when you have drawn that line draw the straight lines across the top of the U.

Aa Bb Cc Dd

Ee Ff Gg Hh

Ii, Jj, Kk,

Ll, Mm, Nn,

Oo, Pp, Qu,

Rr, Ss, Tt,

Uu, Ov, Ww,

Xx, Yy, Zz

This is French Script which is a popular lettering for writing poetry. Or you may prefer the script shown below. Either way, practice each of the alphabets given with large letters and small letters in an exercise book so that you can get accustomed to your pen and ink and become more and more expert and being accurate.

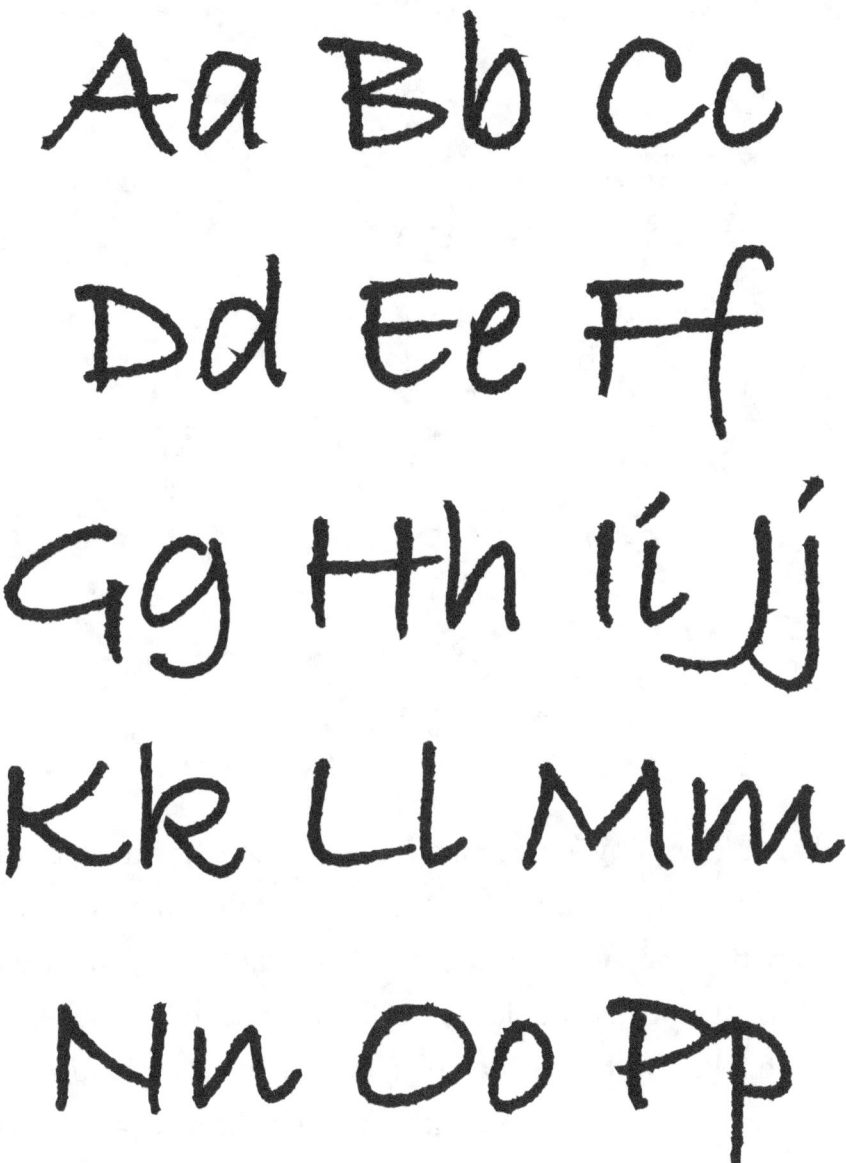

Qq Rr Ss

Tt Uu Vv

Ww Xx Yy

Zz

To begin a scroll, you need a special capital letter to start your work. This is the traditional way to present calligraphy and this is the way that the monks would have used calligraphy to produce hand written books. The idea of calligraphy is to take one single line and follow it through and then another until the whole letter is created. Z can be produced without taking the pen off the paper, as can W, V and other letters, though if there are definite separate lines, then use these as your guide.

Now try practicing writing words using either one of the above alpha bets.

Poetry in Motion

Poetry in Motion

Poetry in Motion

These are very simple examples but there are many printable alphabets that you can download freely from the Internet and these will help you to have a variety of letters that you can copy into your handbook and practice. Just as you learned to write at school, you need to learn again, this time watching the way that your nib moves to create the strokes that make up the letters that you are writing.

0123456789 —
ABCDEFGHIJKLMN
OPQRSTUVWXYZ
abcdefghijklmnop
qrstuvwxyz

In this above example, what you are seeing is an alphabet which uses shadow, but it's a typical style used for calligraphy. For this style, you would most certainly lift your pen before making each stroke. For example, the A is started at the top and the pen is taken down at the correct angle to create the right hand side of the A followed by the left hand side and the tail of the letter and lastly the crossbar. Look at the angles on the letters because this gives you a clue as to where to lift and put down your pen to create similar curves. You can add shadow if you want to lift the letters from the page, though it is suggested that you use pencil to do this in the form of shading.

Use your exercise book regularly, so that you get accustomed to using it because practice really does make perfect. You need to be able to produce large and small letters which perfectly align with each other. The problem that many new calligraphers experience is that they want results too quickly. It is far better to practice those alphabets over and over again, so that when you do start to produce your own calligraphic presentations, you know how the ink flows, you know your own weaknesses and you know which nibs produce which results.

Trying different nibs

This is vital because you may find that other nibs within your set can do a better job at certain elements within your calligraphic work. For example, if you want to produce a series of lines in the background, those lines should be fine. Thus, using the fine nib against a ruler will be necessary. It isn't as easy as it sounds because ink can stain an adjacent area when you move the ruler. Practice it and make sure that your method is solid before trying this on an item you don't want to spoil. Use tissue paper frequently if you think that there is too much ink on the pen nib or the edge of the ruler.

Practice the alphabet over and over and move your pen in the way indicated with the blue lines. Ludwig Tan has kindly drawn this style guide for a complete alphabet on his blog but it's a superb illustration of the movements of the pen as you form your letters.

Practice, practice and practice again because the more you do, the more natural your lettering will be when it really matters. Instead of half-concentrating on copying a style, you will be able to form these letters without having to refer to your book all of the time and when they become natural, it's great fun and very rewarding.

There are several projects that you can use your calligraphy for and these are shown in the chapters to follow. There will of course be other projects that you will think up for yourself, but this is where the fun starts and where you start to actually get to produce something worth keeping. Calligraphy is a worthwhile hobby, so why not use it to create little pieces of time that you made yourself, using the words that you created using pen strokes on parchment.

Sandra Williams

Chapter 5
Producing your first scroll

This is a great idea for presenting poetry or for creating a unique gift you want to give to someone. It could be a certificate of some kind or a thank you letter. It could be a coming of age scroll or a congratulatory scroll. I personally used the Desiderata because it offers words of hope and is a great piece of literature to offer friends.

You will need to have whatever it is that you want to place on the scroll written out because this helps you to decide upon how the scroll needs to be lined in light pencil so that the placement of the letters is accurate and looks neat and tidy. You can rub out the lines once your work is finished. Allow a large space for the first letter of a verse if you are writing poetry, or for each paragraph if you are writing prose.

Things that you will need:

- Pencil – Preferably HB as this can be used lightly and then erased.

- Eraser

- Ruler

- Red ribbon

- Sealing Wax

- Sealing Wax stamp (both of the last items can be bought at an art store)

- Inks

- Calligraphy Pen

- Paper glue

You are best working on a surface like a desk because that slope is perfect for writing and if the desk has a lip, this can hold many of the things that you need during the course of the work. Make sure that you are in good light as this is vital.

Write the complete message that you want to place onto the scroll in your exercise book, so that you know exactly how many words you want. You can also play around with different layouts in your exercise book. The problem with doing the work directly onto the scroll is that you will find at the end of lines that you run out of space for the words you want to add.

Now calculate how many lines there are of script. Leaving a larger space top and bottom, draw that number of lines. This is easy to work out. Leave your space at the top and an equal space at the bottom and measure between the points where you want the space to be left. Divide this by the number of lines you have calculated needing and this will give you the spacing. Mark with a ruler down the sides of the scroll the points where these lines begin and finish and draw them.

To begin your calligraphy, it's usual to have a space for a large letter at the beginning of the work. This is traditional and looks rather nice.

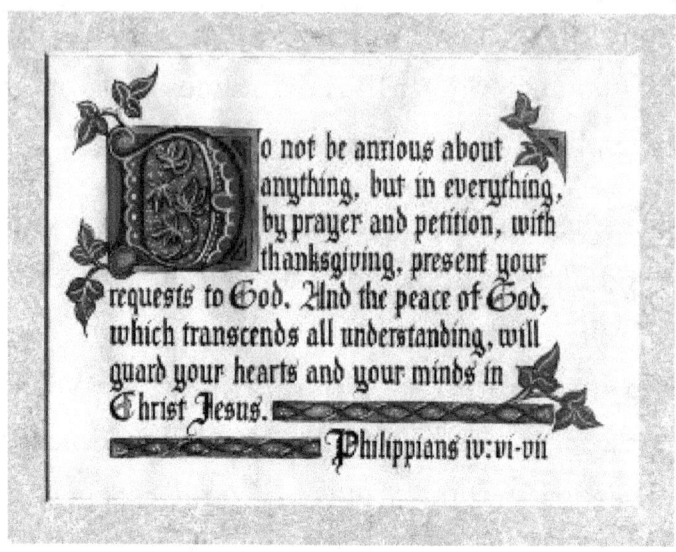

Your work may not be as complex as this, but you see how they left a square at the top for the first letter and embellished it. That's what we are aiming to do.

Creating Lines for Poetry

You need to remember that poems are split into separate verses and for this to appear correctly on your parchment, you will need to have a larger space between verses.

Creating an outline

To create an outline where all your letters will go, you need to lightly draw the letters in pencil. It doesn't have to be in the style of script that you have chosen but the letters should be evenly spaced to give a great layout. This pencil drawing of your letters means that you get to know if you need to tighten up or if you need to make your letters larger. As you write each line, be aware of the space between words and look to see if you run out of space at the end of the line. It doesn't look great if letters are all squashed up. If you find you can't get the right number of words onto the line, erase your pencil letters and make them smaller.

When you have finished penciling in all of your words and are happy that they fit the space correctly, stand back from the work and view it from a distance because sometimes you get a better feel for perspective when you stand back and look at what you have done from a short distance away from the desk.

Now make sure that your desk is clear of everything except your ink, your calligraphy pen, a roll of kitchen tissue and your exercise book. Before you draw the first letter, get a feel for using the ink. Write the first word onto a page of your exercise book and see if you are happy with your lettering. The reason you do this with each word is that it shows you where your weaknesses are and you have a chance to adjust them when you actually write the word onto the parchment.

Parchment is relatively expensive and it's a shame to rush. Remember that the first letter of the first word will be missing because we are going to place this into the square that was created at the beginning. Continue to work in this way until your whole line is created.

Remember: Exercise book word before parchment word.

Moving down the scroll

You need to be very careful with your work and make sure that words that you have already formed are not smudged. If this means taking more time then it is worth it because the picture that you are producing will be perfectly formed letters that can be added to by little flourishes of leaves or flowers in appropriate places once all the words are down on the parchment.

When you are happy with the results of your writing, allow it to dry for 24 hours. Although ink will dry faster than that, you need to be absolutely sure it is perfectly dry before you begin to erase the pencil marks. One smudge could be one smudge too many.

When removing the pencil marks, be very careful working around your letters very gently. A soft eraser is best for this purpose.

Your First Initial Letter

This is the letter that you choose to begin your work. In this case, I have provided several easy examples, but before you attempt to draw them onto your scroll, practice them to scale in your exercise book. If you know that you have a two inch square, draw that in your book so that you are working exactly as you will be on the scroll. As a beginner, it's best that you don't try anything too complex at this stage. The initials below will look stunning and you can add little flowers or leaves if you wish you.

It is essential to practice these. If this means drawing them in pencil and then inking them, that's the best way I found when I started to use more complex lettering for this initial letter on a page. These are shown with good contrast so that you can see them, but of course the background does not have to be yellow! This is more of a drawing of a letter and your drawing should be as accurate as possible. Then add the background afterward, but do it in pencil. Then ink it and it will look beautiful. Although the image shows black lettering and black flora, you can use colors and this is a great time to experiment with colored inks.

Inks can be mixed but your nib should be completely clean each time that you change color. Thus having a jam jar of water available to clean the nib will be useful.

Attaching the ribbon folded in a loop and placing the sealing wax over it for presentation is very easy to do.

Roll the scroll up, once you are sure that everything is in order and that all your pencil markings have been taken off it. Be satisfied with your total scroll and stand back and look at it from a distance. Then roll it up completely. Hold the scroll in that position and place elastic bands that do not squash the roll to keep it in place.

Fold your ribbon or wrap it around the scroll ending with a bow. Then place your sealing wax in a blob over the knot of the ribbon and press your seal into it. It makes a superb gift, thank you or congratulations gift.

Suggested content for scrolls:

- Dad of the Year

- Mom of the Year

- Student of the Year

- Passing Driving Test

- Inspirational scroll

- Birthdays

- Thanksgiving

- Christmas and New Year Resolutions

As you can see, there are a lot of uses that these can be put to and calligraphy is every bit as relevant today as it always was because it means that you put personal effort into your gift instead of opting to buy something ready-made. That makes all the difference to those recipients.

Sandra Williams

Chapter 6

Using a Plume

If you have never tried this, it's well worth the effort. It also gets you back to basics of how calligraphy used to be done. There are several types of quill pen that you can buy and it's best to buy unless you have a lot of time to experiment with feathers from the wild. You can opt for a traditional plume pen or you can be a calligraphy set which is made from a plume and then uses different nibs to in effect cheat a little. It doesn't matter which way you choose to go, but working with a plume which is made from a feather is slightly different from working with calligraphy pens in this day and age.

For one thing, you will find that a quill will be unpredictable in the amount of ink that it holds. The small reservoir of the quill will hold as much ink as you allow it to, but it takes a while to gage it correctly.

Use your exercise book and use black ink and dip the quill into the ink, being aware that the further you dip it, the more ink it is going to hold. At first you will find that the quill is a little scratchy compared to a traditional nib but you can file this down if you find that you want it a different shape or width.

When working with a plume, you hold it as you would a pen but the position of the quill end against the paper is slightly different. Move it at different angles until you find the area of comfort.

If you want to make your own quill, it does take quite a bit of work because not only do you need to find the feathers, but you also need to cut and shape the quill nib and temper it because without this, it won't last very long.

Where to buy ready-made feather quills

These can be found on sites like eBay and what you need to look for is a quill which has a split to take the ink. Look at all of the details. Some sellers have quills but they have simply put a traditional end on them. These will give consistent results but are cheating a little.

If you want to experience a really fine feather quill then look at the details that are listed on the item and read whether the nib is an addition or part of the actual feather stem.

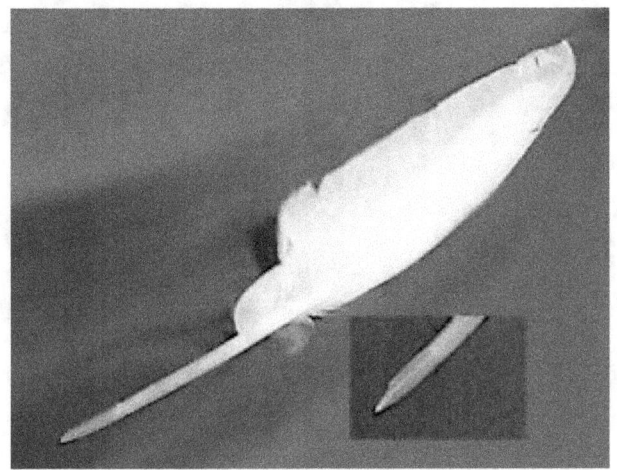

It takes a while to get used to using a quill but any calligrapher worth their salt will give it a go at some stage just to experience what it's like to use these pens. At this stage, while you are just beginning, the quill is a novelty but it may just set the right mood for you to take your calligraphy seriously.

Sandra Williams

Chapter 7

Calligraphy as an Art Form

With calligraphic lettering being so attractive, it's small wonder that people are using it so much for artwork. If you do want to create a work of art to hang in your home, you need to carefully choose the lettering so that it looks the part. As you will be working with larger letters, you need to have either solid colors or have sufficient detail to make the letters look more interesting.

As you upscale with calligraphy, you will be drawing the letters and then coloring them in with either paints or inks. Thus, you will need to make sure that the paper chosen is suitable for water based colors so that your inks or paints do not warp the paper.

Setting out your calligraphy

Sign writers are taught to divide their page into areas where the letters will go. Just as you did with your scroll, you need to work out the mathematics of the layout. How many words? How much space have you got? Is it a poem? Is it a phrase? What size of lettering would you get away with?

When you have worked this out, you need to mark lines on your paper as guides to where the words go and lightly write the words with pencil in ordinary writing but in the size that you will be using to give you a clue where the lettering goes. Be a little bit aware because when you upsize calligraphy, there are certain letters that look wider apart than they actually are so stand back and look at your penciled outline and see if any of the letters need to be moved before actually designing them and painting them.

A great source for calligraphy lettering is Dover Books and although they give no detailed explanation, you don't need it because their books give pages and pages of designs that are copyright free and that you can use in your projects. You can also use the fonts that are available with Word and type the lettering to the size that you want it which will automatically give you the spacing that you need and the size of the letters.

Once you have your item typed in the font that you like, print it. Even if you only have a normal sized printer, you can print sections so that you have all the lettering that you need. Use carbon paper to move these letters onto your artwork but be sure that it's the kind that doesn't leave blot marks.

Then ink in the outlines and wait for the ink to dry if you want to color them in with water color or colored ink or even acrylics. You can add flourishes when the lettering is in place so that's more important for the time being. Once it is all done, add a few leaves and flowers to give your design a little more color and don't forget that you can always use that illuminated first letter and place an artistic frame around your work to give it a real flourish.

Sandra Williams

Chapter 8

Using Calligraphy for Sign-Writing

There is a world of difference between writing down letters on a page and writing a professional sign, though it's worth learning about how this is done because it can be something your calligraphy leads to that will be pleasing. Whether the sign that you write is a house sign, a sign to warn people that you have a dog or simply a sign made for fun, the same rules will apply as they do for calligraphy on paper.

Measurement

Measurement is the first thing that needs to be taken into account. You need to know the size of the sign that you are about to create. This may sound fundamental but it actually makes a lot of difference because this dictates the size of the lettering that you will use and whether there is any space for a border of any kind.

You also need to establish if you want a border as many larger signs do have a simple border just to set the lettering off.

Just as you would do on a piece of artwork, you need proportions worked out and thus having a painted background, start to mark out the lettering that you want to incorporate. You may already have an idea about the type of letting that you want to use, though this time, if it is a font style you will need to work out the size of the lettering to be used. Use the rules on a text document and print one and see if it needs to be increased in size.

As soon as you have all the words printed in the size that you will use, these need to be placed accurately onto your sign. Although there are people who can do this freehand, I have never been able to do this and find that printed fonts work very well indeed.

Use carbon paper to trace the letters onto the board. You will only need to trace around the outlines. If you want some more interesting fonts, there is a very useful site called sign-rite.co.uk which has sets of fonts available suitable for signwriting.

Calligraphic painting

In this case, you need to have chosen your color to contrast sufficiently with the background so that the sign can be clearly seen. You will need several tools for the signwriting process. You will need good quality brushes and there is a gadget that you can make that is traditionally used by sign-writers to help hold their hand steady.

This is made from a piece of thick dowel and you simply wrap painters tape around and around the ends to form a padding. This is held with the left hand, while the right hand leans the paintbrush against the stick for absolute precision and so that the brush does not slip.

A lining fitch is the ideal paintbrush, though you may find that you have your own preferences but practice will show you which brushes are the best for you. Most signs are performed in oil based paints because these are suitable for outdoors.

When working on sign writing, it's easy to forget which part of the sign is wet so you must always work on a set area at a time and work toward you. If this means turning the sign, then that works as well.

Adding extra lines for emphasis

When you are working at this scale, it's easy to introduce shadow or extra lines for emphasis. Shadow adds extra depth to the letters and makes them look very professional.

Image copyright: Creative commons attribution TheDoLittle

Chapter 9

How to Hand Make Popular Fonts

Computers have made life easier for calligraphy lovers. These gadgets can give you hundreds of fonts to imitate, not to mention history about each font and tips on how to hand make some of these popular fonts. Plus, you can also learn the latest trends in calligraphy.

The top ten fonts are definitely useful and beautiful but are not easily replicated. As a beginner, it will be to your advantage if you will start with the simplest font. As you develop your skill and confidence, you can move on to more difficult fonts. For starters, this is how you can hand make or write Helvetica light. This type of font is easy to imitate as the lines are simple and they are void of designs or complicated strokes. Most of the capital letters are straight and for beginners, the lower cases can prove to be challenging enough.

First, purchase or download a lettering guide. This is a piece of paper where the complete alphabet, numbers and other characters written in Helvetica light is written with a space provided for your own handwriting. Letters such as E, F, H, I, L, and T are the easiest to do as they are just straight. The next letters that are easy to make are those with straight and slant lines such as A, K, M, N, V, W, X, and Z. The remaining letters, with curves and rounded, are the hardest to do. As mentioned, lower cases tend to be more difficult to replicate.

Next, find a comfortable table and chair where you could work. A light table is preferable however, if you do not have one, any table will do. Just make sure that the place is well lighted. If this is the case, use a tracing paper. You can also start with a pencil then switch to a pen when you feel ready.

Do air tracing first. This is to familiarize yourself with the shapes, height, and style of each letter or character. Simply draw the letter in the air as if you are already writing it in paper. Practice air tracing until you are ready to do the real thing.

Place the tracing paper on top of the lettering guide. Sit down properly. Position your dominant hand comfortably on the table. Start tracing the upper cases. Usually, there is a space provided to practice this for three or four times. Do not worry if your handwriting is squiggly or if you commit an error. Just continue until you finish the set. Pause and check your work. Look where you missed it or where you had difficulty. Try to do air practice again. Repeat the procedure for the upper cases.

Proceed with the lower cases. Do the same as with the upper cases. Then, trace the numbers and remaining characters. Most lettering guides have sentences that you can trace, too. This will give you the opportunity to practice everything that you have learned in one line or two.

Get another tracing paper and repeat the procedure. Finally, when you have mastered the letters and you feel that you can do it without the aid of the lettering guide and the tracing paper, then proceed with the actual handwriting. However, one is encouraged to use either a graph or ruled paper first. Write the upper cases on the graph paper. Check your work. If you are satisfied, continue the process. If you feel you need more time with tracing the letters, go back to that process. As they say, perfect practice makes perfect.

After several practice sessions, you can proceed on actual handwriting. This time, use a clean, blank paper. Do not trace. Just write the letters on the paper using the same sequence – upper cases, lower cases, numbers, and the remaining characters. Next, practice with sentences. Again, practice as much as you can until it looks great.

The steps for handwriting script and more complicated fonts are actually the same as above. The difference maybe will be on the time spent for practice as these types would require more practice hours before you can master them thoroughly.

This is the traditional method. Today, one has the advantage of advanced technology to aid him or her in learning the art of calligraphy easily. Plus, do you know that you can actually convert your own handwriting into fonts that you can use for your personal invitations, memos, projects, or letters? How is this done? Get your handwriting on the screen of your computer using tools like MyscriptFont.com or PaintFont.com. You will be asked to fill their template using your own handwriting. Scan the finished template, save and submit. Follow the step-by-step procedure. That's it! You can use your own font anytime you want.

There are other things you can do to improve your skills. The bottom line though is practice. You can master any font using these steps any time. It all depends on you. There is no difficult font that you cannot conquer through sheer patience and practice.

Practice decorative font as well for the use in the opening of your calligraphy just like they used to do when books were written by monks. Some of the letters that you learn to draw are amazingly detailed but are a great way of adding color to your creations. Learn different methods of intertwining floral decoration to a letter as this helps as well and you're opening letter doesn't have to be that complex. Simple designs work too.

Get in touch with others who are interested in calligraphy online and share your experience with others, because this helps you to expand upon your own knowledge base at the same time, sharing ideas so that you can produce great quality lettering with a lot of imagination and flare.

Sloping letters

You need to get accustomed to keeping the slope of your letters nice and even. It's a great idea to write within lines and having drawn a grid in pencil helps to keep your slope uniform when you start to do calligraphy. However, with experience, you will find that keeping the slope regular will become easier and that you no longer need these grids, except when doing large lettering such as on signwriting projects.

The construction of popular fonts is usually very straightforward. The down strokes are usually the widest strokes and if you draw spiraling patterns you will see how the calligraphy pen nib responds at different angles or as you turn a corner on your design. It becomes quite easy after a while.

Try some swirls and watch how the pen changes the thickness of the lines as this is all part and parcel of using calligraphy pens.

There are literally thousands of different types, but just practicing the swirls is good for calligraphic practice because they are decorative elements that you can add to your work and which add a great element of decoration as well as improving your penmanship techniques.

Chapter 10
Calligraphy and Financial Gains

Although computers have revolutionized the art of calligraphy, more people still prefer the traditional and more personal touch of actual handwriting. Hence, the business side of calligraphy will automatically get in you even though that is not your original intention. When you become good in calligraphy and people start seeing your work, orders or tutorial lesson offers are not far behind.

Here are some of the ways you can have extra income with calligraphy.

- Be a tutor. This is a good way to enjoy your newfound hobby and earn at the same time. Most people do not have the time or patience to learn calligraphy by themselves or to teach their children. You can post an ad or just inform your friends or acquaintances of your skill and rate as a tutor. Plus, you can also sell calligraphy materials and earn from that. Simply add a markup and you can even make that as a package – tutorial with calligraphic paraphernalia included. A good strategy is to offer a free calligraphy seminar to kids for one day. Parents usually grab these offers and when their kids show potentials at this new skill, they would not hesitate to sign you up to teach their kids.

- Do projects for a fee. Weddings and event invitations use calligraphy even in this modern time. There is a magical appeal to the actual beautiful handwriting compared to the perfect result of a printed font. One can also do logo designs, graphic arts, religious designs, and other calligraphic arts. The possibilities are endless.

- Cake designs. Getting popular nowadays are personalized themed cakes. Having calligraphic skills is an advantage. This requires advanced skill however as the actual handwriting is done as the last part so an error would result to the loss of the whole cake. However, when one is skilled enough, even an error in handwriting could be remedied with drawings or decors or a slight stroke here and there.

- T-shirt designing plus more. Another good business idea is the combination of apparel and calligraphy.

Personalized shirts become more beautiful and unique when an actual handwriting is used. This could be used as tokens for family gatherings or other intimate celebrations. It is also a great gift suggestion during special holidays or occasions. It could also be used in skirts, pants, socks, or even shoes.

- Bags and accessories. Yes. You can also do calligraphy on bags, belts, headbands, lanyards, and basically any accessory that you can think of. There is a special paint that you can use that would stick to these items.

- Home decors. Do you know that you can handwrite a bible verse or a famous quotation, frame, sell and earn from it? Something that requires very minimal capital could give you a handsome profit.

Plus so much more! There is indeed a huge market for calligraphers. All businesses or companies would require the services of a calligrapher at least once in their existence. Calligraphy and business go hand in hand. There is money in calligraphy. From sign-writing to actually producing awards for employees, companies are interested in the work that you can produce and you may find that you will be able to make a reasonable amount of money from your hobby.

This section of the book has shown you how to produce calligraphy letters, and how to use them for decoration or for the simple satisfaction of producing beautiful presentation. However, it's worth considering that you may find people with less patience than you who are prepared to buy your work on sites like Etsy or eBay, especially if you make things that are suitable for birthdays and occasions that they want to celebrate. People pay good money for work that is well done.

Chapter 11
The Future of Calligraphy

As the world is pushing for a paperless generation, the future for calligraphy may seem dim, too. On the contrary, however, there is a rich future awaiting this art. Technology has made life easier for mankind. That is true. For instance, when it comes to calligraphy, an error cannot be easily remedied unlike in computer where you would just press the delete button and start again. A work of calligraphy can take hours compared to minutes or even seconds with computers. The results with these high tech gadgets would always be perfect. One cannot expect to have the same results with actual handwriting. Still, calligraphy is expected to thrive and even flourish as the years come. Why?

Here are some reasons for the continued existence of calligraphy hundreds and even thousands of years from now.

- Art is forever. Time has proven over and over again how a form of art could exist amidst chaos, changes, difficulty, or even advancement in technology and life in general. Mankind will not lose its love for beautiful things and creations. You would see that in how much value and care are given to other forms of arts such as paintings, sculptures, monuments, writings, to name just a few

- Calligraphy makes things more personal and humane. Compare a computer printed invitation to that of a handwritten one. Would you feel the person's warmth and sincerity more in the former or the latter? Undeniably, calligraphy will win every time. You would feel the labor of love in each letter. You would sense the effort and time spent in making that invitation, which in turn would make you feel special. It may not be as perfect as the printed invitation but somehow you would find the handwritten invitation more beautiful and appealing.

- Words are eternal. Unless mental telepathy would be as natural as breathing in the ages to come, man would always resort to words as a form of communication. Hence, calligraphy will not cease its existence. It will only do so when men stop communicating with one another, which is an impossible thing to occur. Life is made up of words. Therefore, as long as there is life, there would be words. As long as there are words, there would be letters.

As long as there are letters, there would always be calligraphy.

A paperless generation is possible; however, a *calligraphy-less* generation is not. Why? Calligraphy is not limited to paper alone. One will never run out of ideas where to handwrite their thoughts, feelings, ideas, and passion. Hence, the future of calligraphy is already written – it is definitely here to stay.

Go through all the stages and steps shown within the pages of this book and you can really use your skills to make something very worthwhile. Start small and as you gain confidence, you will be able to take on larger projects and learn more about more advanced calligraphy practice as you go.

You can also create projects for your children so that they are sure to pass on this craft to their kids in turn. The writing of words is important and the calligraphy that people do today is something that is writing a history all of its own. The birthday greetings, the congratulations certificates or even the sign that shows people where the local vet's office is are all part of 21st century calligraphy and when you learn how to do it, you will find yourself very keen to increase your knowledge and try different kinds of lettering. You will be pleased with the work that you do, but the next time, you will be even more pleased because the experience is a valuable one and you improve all of the time.

Sandra Williams

Chapter 12

Choosing Appropriate Styles for Your Project

The reason that I have suggested that you have some text books for your calligraphy is because of the wide range of styles that is available. You only get to know which styles are suitable for your projects by knowing what styles there are and having these source books will really help you to have a broader view. In the Dover range alone, there are over a dozen books covering different styles.

Calligraphy isn't something that you will leave you thinking you know it all because of the number of styles available. For example, if you want to write a scroll, you need to choose a style of writing that's easy to read and that suits the occasion. For a certificate of merit of some kind, you need that format to be fairly formal so that the person receiving it feels that it's the certificate or scroll that you have made has been tailored to fit the occasion.

Poetry can be written in styles that are flowing so that they go along with the sentiment of the poem and it's very much a personal choice what kind of calligraphy style you choose. I tend to go for flowery patterns for poetry until the poetry is of a serious nature and then I tend to use more formal calligraphy styles.

I always use a larger letter at the beginning of paragraphs because it adds the potential of colors and the Dover book of monograms is a great source book for these. You may even find monograms on Pinterest and these can be used to give you new ideas for your initial that starts your work off.

Your drawing skills will improve and if you fear drawing and want to start your work with very detailed initials, you can always use the ones from your source book and then blow them up to the size that you require. On one initial that I wanted for a particularly flowery project I was doing, the design that I chose from a source book was so delicate and interwoven that I was incapable of actually copying it, but I was capable of reproducing it.

Using your scanner, scan the image into your computer and then size it by opening it up as an image in Word and stretching to the appropriate size. Print it. Then you are able to trace it using tracing paper and pencil the back of the design over the lines that you have drawn. Turn it around to the right way out and place it where you need it on your paper. Hold it in place using painter's tape as this won't affect the surface of the paper and is easy to remove. I usually run my hand over the sticky side before using it. It retains enough stickiness to keep the image in place and then comes off the paper easily when you have finished. Now take a biro pen and follow the lines on your chosen drawing and the pencil on the back of the image will leave an impression.

This kind of tracing becomes very easy after a while and I use it a lot to place the initial letter on a lot of the work that I do. That way, even if your drawing skills are limited, you can still produce first class initials and your work will look great.

If you are making signs for a business or a sign for your home, then remember that legibility is paramount. Thus avoid using lettering that is too complex such as Old English. Some people really do have problems reading this kind of text. You are safer sticking with Times New Roman or Book Antiqua because these are a lot easier for people to read.

You can have a little artistic license if you are designing something that is primarily thought of as art. Some of the illumination letters that are found in Holy books make great letters to start a chapter, and when you draw these, you could even add a little gold to the edges.

The way that I do this is by using an acrylic gold paint and a very fine paintbrush, but first you create the lettering and the edging is done afterwards so that the lines of the edging are crisp and clean. I experimented with my initial letter to begin a chapter and found that lining lead, which is sold in a tube can be very good for the outline of that letter, since you can use your nib and colored inks to color in the letter once the lead lining has dried.

Experiment. Seek out new ideas at your craft center because there are so many calligraphy goodies hiding away on the shelves of stores and you may even find that they have a whole host of sheets of different styles of lettering all ready for people like you who want to learn calligraphy.

If not, look online in Google Images to find downloadable and printable sheets of different scripts because it's good to make your own source book so that you have plenty to choose from with each project that you begin. I have sheets of different styles that I downloaded and these are kept in an art folder because the lettering is suitable for large projects and I know that I can always dip into that folder and find a lot of inspiration when I have a new calligraphy project to undertake. Think of the project – then check out the styles and choose the appropriate style to suit the project you are about to undertake.

Sandra Williams

Conclusion

Thank you again for purchasing this book!

I hope this book was able to help you to become a successful calligrapher or at least make a start at becoming one. There are always going to be a great deal of designs and finding new ones to suit new projects is always something that's easy to do, with the potential of the Internet and websites such as Pinterest. You will also find supplies and ideas for new projects from people who, like you, are enjoying the art and are willing to pass on their ideas.

The next step is to enjoy this newfound skill or even profit from it by starting your own calligraphy business or work as a calligrapher. If you are not that ambitious and just want to do calligraphy as a hobby, that's valuable too. Imagine being able to make a journal that is all done in calligraphy. It would make a wonderful souvenir. Some parents even make baby books with the use of calligraphy to pass on to their children when they are grown up and have kids of their own.

Finally, if you enjoyed this book, please take the time to share your thoughts and post a review on Amazon. It'd be greatly appreciated!

Thank you and good luck!

www.ingramcontent.com/pod-product-compliance
Lightning Source LLC
Chambersburg PA
CBHW071220280526
45787CB00002B/747